THIS CANDLEWICK BOOK BELONGS TO:

_____

_____

_____

For Agnes from me, and for
Holly from the elephants
*M. J.*

For all of George's grandmas:
Hazel, Kathy, Pauline, and Gillian
*I. B.*

Text copyright © 2003 by Martin Jenkins
Illustrations copyright © 2003 by Ivan Bates

First paperback edition 2007

The Library of Congress has cataloged the hardcover edition as follows:

Jenkins, Martin.
Grandma Elephant's in charge / Martin Jenkins ;
illustrated by Ivan Bates. —1st U.S. ed.
p. cm.
Summary: Describes the behavior of elephants in a family group, particularly the
role of the older female elephants.
ISBN 978-0-7636-2074-5 (hardcover)
1. Elephants—Behavior—Juvenile literature. 2. Familial behavior in animals—
Juvenile literature. [1. Elephants. 2. Familial behavior in animals.] I. Bates, Ivan, ill.
II. Title.
QL737.P98 J46 2003
599.67—dc21      2002073439

ISBN 978-0-7636-3285-4 (paperback)

10 9 8 7 6 5 4 3 2 1

Printed in China

This book was typeset in Cheltenham and Shinn.
The illustrations were done in watercolor and colored pencil.

Candlewick Press
2067 Massachusetts Avenue
Cambridge, Massachusetts 02140

visit us at www.candlewick.com

# GRANDMA ELEPHANT'S IN CHARGE

Martin Jenkins

illustrated by
Ivan Bates

CANDLEWICK PRESS
CAMBRIDGE, MASSACHUSETTS

**M**ost elephants live in families.
And most elephant
families are **big**
(just like elephants).

Elephants are the biggest land animals of all. A big male can weigh more than six tons — as much as 100 people.

**T**here'll probably be two or three babies,
forever playing push-me-pull-you, or peekaboo,
or anything else that makes a lot of noise.
And each of the babies might have an older brother
or sister—handy for playing king-of-the-mountain on!

Elephant mothers have only one baby at a time.
They give birth every three or four years.
Elephants don't become fully grown until
they're ten years old or more.

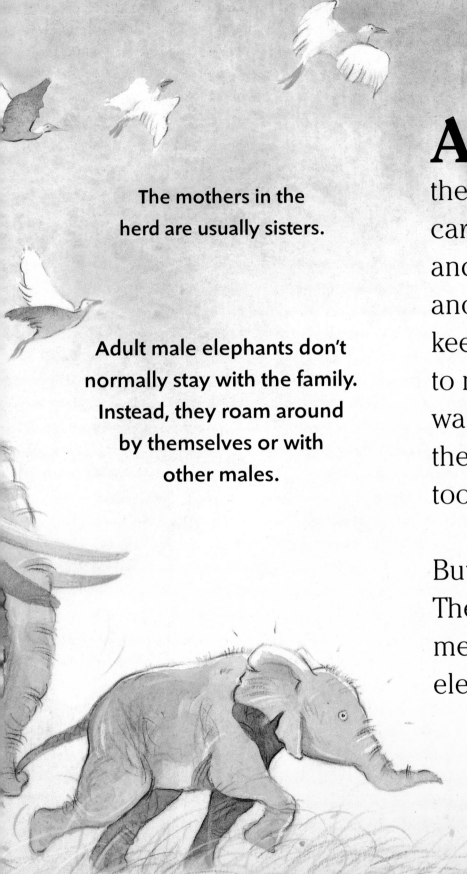

**The mothers in the herd are usually sisters.**

**Adult male elephants don't normally stay with the family. Instead, they roam around by themselves or with other males.**

**A**nd then there are the moms. They take care of their own babies and help with one another's too— keeping an eye on them to make sure they don't wander off, and scolding them when they get too boisterous.

But that's not all. The most important member of an elephant family is . . .

# Grandma!

Elephants can live for up to sixty-five years but don't usually have any more babies once they're older than fifty or so.

Grandma's been around a long time and she knows lots of important things. She knows where the water holes are when it hasn't rained and the easiest places to cross the big river when it has rained.

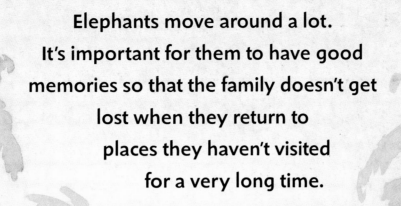

Elephants move around a lot.
It's important for them to have good
memories so that the family doesn't get
lost when they return to
places they haven't visited
for a very long time.

She knows where to find the juiciest melons…
and knows the best path up the cliff to the salt lick.
It's not surprising that she's the one in charge.

Elephants are very fond of things like melons but feed mainly on grass, leaves, and twigs. Adults eat about 350 pounds of food each day.

Salt licks are places where the earth is full of minerals. Lots of animals eat the salty earth there, which helps to keep them healthy.

She doesn't make a big
song and dance about
it, though. Just a flick of
the ear or a snort or two,
and a **rumble,**
**rumble,**
**rumble,** deep
down in her throat, seem
to be enough to tell all
the other elephants
what to do.

If she stops, they all stop.
If she moves, they all move.
And if there's any sign
of danger, you can be
sure she'll be the first to
investigate and the first
to decide what the
family should do.

They might all run away…
or they might take a stand.

Or Grandma might **c-h-a-r-g-e**.
If she charges with her head up and ears
flapping, waving her trunk and making
a great hullabaloo, then she's probably bluffing.

But if her head's down, her trunk's
tucked under, and she's not making
any noise, then she means business.
In that case, whoever it is that has
annoyed her had better watch out.

**A charging elephant can
run 25 miles an hour — that's faster
than the fastest human.**

And once all the commotion's over,
everyone can settle back down to feeding
and snoozing and messing around—
knowing that Grandma has sorted
things out again.

So if you're an elephant, there's one thing you should never forget. Wherever you are and whatever you're doing,

# Grandma's in charge!

# ABOUT ELEPHANTS

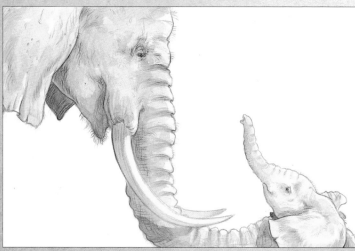

There are two kinds of living elephants. The elephants in this book are African elephants; the other kind are Asian elephants, which live in South and Southeast Asia. Elephants were once found almost everywhere in Africa, but now they have disappeared from many of the places where they used to live. This is because they have been hunted and people have taken their land for farming. Twenty years ago, there were more than one million African elephants. Now there may be only half that number.

## INDEX

Look up the pages to find out about all these elephant things. Don't forget to look at both kinds of words—
this kind and this kind.

## MARTIN JENKINS

is a conservation biologist who works for agencies such as the World Wide Fund for Nature and the World Conservation Monitoring Centre. Explaining his fascination with elephants, he says "I first saw wild elephants in the Masai Mara National Reserve in Kenya. There was a big family of them, making their way across the savanna. I've seen elephants lots of times since then, but I'll never forget that first family, strolling across the plains without a care in the world—it was magic."

## IVAN BATES

has illustrated many books for children, including *Do Like a Duck Does!* by Judy Hindley and three books by Sam McBratney—*The Dark at the Top of the Stairs, Just You and Me,* and *Just One.* Ivan Bates says of *Grandma Elephant's in Charge,* "I have always found elephants fascinating creatures, capable of both extreme strength and tenderness. This, along with their mighty stature and wonderful habitat of vast landscapes and skyscapes, makes them a joy to draw."